Fire from the Heart
2021

Winners of the 2021 Muriel's Journey Poetry Prize

THREE OCEAN PRESS

All poems and text © 2021 by their respective authors.

All rights reserved. No part of this publication may be reproduced, stored in a retrieval system, or transmitted, in any form or by any means, electronic, mechanical, photocopying, recording, or otherwise, without prior written permission of the publisher.

All characters in this book are fictional. Any resemblance to persons living or dead is purely coincidental.

Library and Archives Canada Cataloguing in Publication
Title: Fire from the heart, 2021 : winners of the 2021 Muriel's Journey Poetry Prize
Other titles: Winners of the 2021 Muriel's Journey Poetry Prize
Identifiers: Canadiana (print) 20210352396 | Canadiana (ebook) 2021035240X |
ISBN 9781988915388 (softcover) | ISBN 9781988915395 (EPUB)
Subjects: LCSH: Canadian poetry—21st century. | CSH: Canadian poetry (English)—21st century. | LCGFT: Poetry.
Classification: LCC PS8293.1 .F576 2021 | DDC C811/.608—dc23

Editor: Kyle Hawke
Cover and Book Designers: Kyle Hawke and PJ Perdue
Cover art: Journey's End V ©2021 Wade Edwards

Three Ocean Press
8168 Riel Place
Vancouver, BC, V5S 4B3
778.321.0636
info@threeoceanpress.com
www.threeoceanpress.com

First publication, December 2021

Muriel's Journey

The Muriel's Journey Poetry Prize is in its third year! It feels like Muriel's spirit keeps cheering us on, eyes sparkling, arms extended in a wide, warm welcome. This year's contest had vigorous participation from Vancouver's Dowtown Eastside, where I first met Muriel, a place avoided by some because many people there live in great poverty and use alcohol and other substances more openly than in other places. But the DTES is also a thriving, bubbling community where creative juices flow freely and where people give of themselves and to each other with warm and open hearts.

Many, many thanks to Kyle Hawke, my co-organizer, who also put in the labour of love to edit and publish this chapbook. Equally, thanks go to the judges Elee Kraljii Gardiner, Bill Arnott, and Wanda Kewehin-John; to Wade Edwards who donated the cover art; to Glenn Mori, who administered the incoming poems; to Danielle LaFrance, who was the master of ceremonies for the award ceremony; and to the Vancouver Public Library and Word Vancouver, who sponsored the award ceremony.

Isabella Mori
on the traditional, ancestral and unceded territory of the S<u>k</u>w<u>x</u>wú7mesh (Squamish), Səlílwətaʔ/Selilwitulh (Tsleil-Waututh) and xʷməθkʷəy̓əm (Musqueam) Nations
(Vancouver, BC, Canada)

About the Prize

Muriel was a social justice activist, poet, and spoken word artist of Indigenous heritage from the Gitxsan nation's Owl Clan who spent a lot of time in the Downtown Eastside. In her work, she always explored new ways of expressing herself, always talked and wrote about what's urgent and important. Her energy was like fireworks, and her hugs legendary.

Muriel died in November of 2018. At Muriel's memorial at the DTES' Listening Post, someone related that on her last day, Muriel said that while she was leaving, she was still continuing her journey. The text was accompanied by a picture of the sunrise on the day she died. Isabella was moved by this to do their part in Muriel's continued journey, and decided to start a poetry prize in Muriel's honour.

Everyone liked Muriel. She encouraged creative people of all stripes to continue on their path of creativity and social justice, and with Muriel's Journey poetry prize, we hope to pass on inspiration and strength to all who create with a sense of justice in mind.

Because Muriel always did things a little differently, we're doing this poetry prize adifferently, too. Being keenly aware of how subjective the judging of poetry can be, we give a prize to a poet randomly selected from the longlist of those who met the entry requirement of "lively, outspoken ideas ... speak your mind and let the world know what you think ... look at your subject in an unexpected way ... take a risk in your composition ... be frank and unreserved." Another change is our "entry fee," which consists of people showing how they contribute to their community. Lastly, we have two first prizes, a general one and one specifically for a poet with close ties to the Downtown Eastside.

All poems in this collection were submitted and subsequently were selected by judges as the winners of the second annual Muriel's Journey Poetry Prize.

Prizes were awarded at a ceremony on September 20, 2021 via Zoom as part of the Word Vancouver literary arts festival. The ceremony was hosted from the traditional and unceded territory of the Musqueam, Squamish, and Tsleil-Watuth peoples, but included winners reading from their home territories, as noted in their Community Involvement statements at the end of this book.

Organizers
Isabella Mori
Kyle Hawke

Ceremony MC
Danielle LaFrance

Judges
Bill Arnott
Wanda John-Kehewin
Elee Kraljii Gardiner

Special thanks to the Vancouver Public Library and to to Glenn Mori, who administered the poems as they came in. Thanks also to Cecily Nicholson, Diane Wood, and past organizer Rudolf Penner, without whom this whole project would have never happened.

The Muriel's Journey Poetry Prize honours the vitality, vivacity, and outspoken presence of poet-activist Muriel Marjorie, who passed on in the fall of 2018. An Indigenous social justice activist, poet, and spoken word artist, what Muriel had to say would often literally wake you up. Her enthusiastic encouragement of innovative creative endeavours was infectious.

The Muriel's Journey Poetry Prize is open to all residents of Canada and to Canadians living abroad. No submission fee is charged; instead, those entering are asked to provide a statement of their community involvement to demonstrate their active effort to improve the world around them. First prize is $100. The DTES prize is also $100 and celebrates poets with a deep connection to Vancouver's Downtown Eastside. Second prize is $50. One randomly selected poem will receive $35. Judges look for lively, outspoken texts that present ideas in unexpected ways.

For information on the Muriel's Journey Poetry Prize, please contact the organizers at poetryprize@murielsjourney.com or visit their Facebook page.

www.murielsjourney.com

Contents

FIRST PRIZE WINNER
Catherine Garrett
Ruth and Naomi 1

DOWNTOWN EASTSIDE PRIZE WINNER
Dolores Dallas
Grandchild 4

SECOND PRIZE WINNER
Michelle Poirier Brown
A Cure for Sorrow, a Prescription for Despair 5

RANDOM SELECTION
joseph a. farina
Autumnal 6

HONOURABLE MENTIONS
Catherine Garrett
Uncanny Valley 7

Val Davidson
Just Another Day 9

Jano Klimas
Pink Socks 10

Sebastian Yūe
Give Me a Sign 11

Gilles Cyrenne
No No No No No 12

Michelle Poirier Brown
Before the Open Refrigerator Door 13

Winners' Community Involvement 14

Judges' Biographies 17

Judges' Statement 17

First Prize Winner
Ruth and Naomi
Catherine Garrett

they say what you don't know can't hurt you
so I look the other way when he takes my shirt off

the man on tinder asks me:
"so in what way are you bisexual?"
says you don't look non-binary
& suddenly

I am just a confused woman
pulling out pronouns for a party trick

do not urge me to leave you, to turn my back and not follow you

he calls me beautiful

tells me to say his name when I don't know mine
& he does not ask

he marvels at how much of me he can fit in his fists

if I am uncomfortable, we can stop
my breasts are in his hands

this could be called a prayer
both of us brought to our knees

& just tonight
my gender leaves the room when I turn off the lights
but he can't tell the difference

I let him call me
woman
is such a heavy word
but I seem to only have to explain that to the men

over

I first read the story of Ruth and Naomi in kindergarten
I didn't know why I liked it
maybe it's the thought of seeing
& being seen
but not having to question

he asks
if I like it
& his clumsy hands shake

the *yes* from my mouth like baby teeth
I say *yes*
forget myself
say *yes* and mean it
until tomorrow
until he comes

retraumatization looks a lot like desire when you hold it up to the light
three thousand years later my love is still the same
I have spent 24 years thinking I have to lie to be loved

woman   or attention seeker

mentally ill   or faking it

too afraid of the empty side of my bed to tell the truth
but I change the pronouns on my social media
lighting a candle for a loved one

Ruth welcomes Naomi into her house after she lost her husband and two
    children
together / the two women chased the grief from each other's bones
history names them friends
memory will call them destiny

Ruth promises Naomi she will stay with her always
I go out on every first date dressed for a funeral

my mom wants grandkids
my dad refuses to learn pronouns

your people shall be my people & your god shall be my god

two women who braid their stories together into legends
born in different countries
still somehow can't breathe without sharing the same space
Ruth prays to the stars & whispers Naomi's name like a constellation
Naomi's bottom lip trembles & Ruth's ribcage turns to dust
these two/proof that the word love/sounds the same in every language

*because where you will die, I will die too
& there I will be buried*

I don't tell my parents about my first girlfriend until after we break up
I tell a tinder date I prefer they-she pronouns before I tell my mother

*thus and more may the Lord do to me
if anything but death parts me from you*

the same word used to describe how Adam loved Eve
is used for Ruth's Old Testament feelings for Naomi

she is alive again in the words of wedding vows centuries later
& with these words in mind
I decide to do myself the justice of finally being honest

otherwise
when my family finally gets me in a wedding dress
I'm afraid it will be an exorcism

& not a celebration

DOWNTOWN EASTSIDE PRIZE WINNER
Grandchild
Dolores Dallas

Grandchild, when you were just a little one
You lived here with me
This is your land,
this is your home
Your mom, aunties and uncle too
All went to kuper island
Residential school
There was nothing I could say or do
That's what my granny said
Your mom never came home again
She married and lived downtown in vancouver
One day a social worker took you away
From your mom, your dad, and me
Your mom died in jail
Down in the states somewhere
She's buried in a pauper's grave
Unmarked

Your daddy died in a car crash
That's what my granny said
Tears rolled down
Her soft wrinkled face
As she recalled her pain
We hugged and cried for both our loss
Then she whispered to me
We are of the salmon people
We been given many journeys

Some very long , some very hard
But we always return
To our place of birth
Cedar, Sage, and Sweetgrass
Sang their sweet song for you
To celebrate your journey home
That's what my granny said

Second Prize Winner
A Cure for Sorrow, a Prescription for Despair
Michelle Poirier Brown

Change what you wear. Slowly.
Learn to dress for the weather,
one garment at a time.
Wrap your hair with silk
against the sun.
Find a beautiful summer hat—
shelter in illusion.
Use your good taste as a fence.
Unless you don't care,
no longer feel embarrassed.
Unless you've decided
it's time.
Know the temperature at which you change coats.
Love the child of your body.
Buy the shoe you are willing to wear
if you are found dead.
Buy well-made socks.

Near-empty the drawer of rubber bands and twist ties.
More will come.

Throw these away, too.

Eat the things you like, eat them buttered,
with salt and pepper only.
Every day.

Look out the window often and for long stretches.

Allow yourself flowers in vases,
live alongside the spread and bend of tulips.

Wash your face in roses.

Random Selection
Autumnal
joseph a. farina

rain falls
a gentle hand
revealing
dust laid dreams
of ancient shores
i looked to the river then
its slow ease lapping
the cool stones —
i envied them
under the zenith heat
of the noon day sun
waiting for the paper truck
i waited and spoke with the waters
my days were raptor flights
on never ending thermals
of kit kat licking fingers
drinking water from some sprinkler
as i thirsted on the beach road
summer scented — fresh cut grass
and sea smells — along Lake Huron's shore
under the blue skies
under the young sun
i sang the early noon
i lived and feasted on the air
my eyes cataloging
those high days
retrievable now only
through sentiment and wine
or when a gentle rain
falls on the face
of an old man weeping

HONOURABLE MENTION
Uncanny Valley
Catherine Garrett

The fear of something that falls between almost and fully human
is believed to be a natural aversion.

Example: anthropology says homo sapiens killed off other species of
 almost humans
This v e s t i g i a l uneasiness is thought to be as honest as blood can be.
Think dolls, computer ai, robots, and in this case, me. all homunculi

The Uncanny Valley is what happens when you are stuck in shades of grey
Hypothesized relationship to the degree of an object's resemblance to a
 human
Then the emotional response.

When I try and push my best friend's cousin off me, my hands pass
 through him like smoke.
I am the sketched spectre left over after you try and erase the pencil
 marks.
Watching this unfold from the outside, I am human.
 but too drunk to do anything about it.
He… is human, too.

They say whoever commits such an act of violence is a type of beast.
I will tell you he looked like a person for every moment I was with him.
They call the man a *demon* as if I should have noticed the distinction.

Did he really rape me if I didn't recognize myself while he was doing it?
New Year's Day 2016 and I am in the ER
Trying to bridge the gap between almost and completely
My group of friends and I pretend this never happened.

When my mother goes to confront him, he says I wanted it to her face.
I refuse to do a kit because it feels like overreacting, but I know
 something is wrong.
His aunt does not know this when she says *I bet you've had a shower.*

over

*Things like this aren't supposed to happen in small towns, we keep each
    other safe here*
just because you regret it doesn't make it what you're calling it

The concept suggests humanoid objects imperfectly resembling human
    beings
provoke uncanny or strangely familiar feelings of revulsion among
    observers.

The hands are the only thing I can remember properly.
I won't look myself in the mirror for months.
My mother calls this a defence mechanism.
I tell her it's respecting the dead.

Ariana Brown says it takes love to name the damage on one's own body.
I just let it rest before trying to find the words.

HONOURABLE MENTION
Just Another Day
Val Davidson

My *dad* looked so cool
Walking us to school
Buckskin and beads
Ponytail hung long
planting the seeds.

Mother doing dishes
Singing at the sink
Joplin, Dylan, have another drink.

Try and fight the pain
That's driving her insane…
memories that last hidden from her past.

Rich man, poor man, Indian Chief… residential schools and all the racist grief.

Sometimes I think about them, wishing they were here
To wipe away the shame
the pain and the fear.

Rounders and addicts sitting at the table
Knowing the china white is so unstable

Fix another pill
watching him turn blue
Being only 12, what were we to do!

Policemen, junkies
Standing all around
Gunshots fired
hands on the ground.

No one understands it…
it's just another day
Teacher says hello
Dad walks away.

Honourable Mention
Pink Socks
Jano Klimas

what brings me here isn't a desire for fame and prestige
or the lure of the spotlight

what brings me here is narrow and easy
a humming bird and moon light
his wings and the moon's energy

what brings me here are years of searching for peace
the question I can't get rid of
the stars, pelicans and the endless sea

what brings me here is my own action as I swim on the edge of fate
a longing for connection, for warm hand, tea and some biscuits

what brings me here are my pink socks and brown scarpa shoes
I would never have thought of wearing pink socks
but here I am pulling them higher on my shin

what brings me here is the echo of these words
a silent repetition, here, here, here
bring, bring, bring
bring me here where I need to be
what keeps me alive gives meaning to my end

Honourable Mention
Give Me a Sign
Sebastian Yūe

The day I came into the world
there were no bodies, neither astral nor mortal, present
to mark the time and date.

The day I came into the world
the stars stood still,
no celestial celebration for a baby born in a Chinese gutter.

The sun was down and the clouds masked the moon
and I guess heaven's herald was off that day,
I like to think they were on a tropical holiday somewhere nice.

With no sidereal map to orient
and no way to chart a path
I wander from point to point,
connect the dots,
draw my own constellations across quadrants
and hang my destiny
like a corpse
in the sky.

In the vast expanse of the galaxy,
I'll claim space
not caring what coulda, woulda, shoulda been written in the stars

Because after I go supernova,
the sky'll be too dark to read

HONOURABLE MENTION
No No No No No
Gilles Cyrenne

You come to my door with a gift of
memories of
    stuff you've "borrowed" from me
my favourite sweater
my raingear jacket
Swiss army knife
sleeping bag
favourite bowl
multi-bit screwdriver
leather jacket
and you ask me empty-handed
to let you in again
Life on the crack and down streets
is too crazy again
    and you need
three days' sleep
a decent meal
and when I say no
you cry you're cold and wet
with nowhere else to go
So I've a housemate again
for a day or three or so
Until again the streets bid you go
until you return again
to one who can't say no

Honourable Mention
Before the Open Refrigerator Door
Michelle Poirier Brown

It is worn ground, this question:
Fruit or vegetable?

The icons on the drawers are clear:
tap roots, flowerets, and balls of leaf
  (although, actually, leaves of any kind,
      and any sort of plant that might, had it not been picked, have
        blossomed,
            green onions, say)
they are all—icon indicated
  or not—
vegetables.

Fruit follows flower.

It is a question of preservation,
this apprehension of flesh.

Tomatoes in a bowl keep them
from mealiness.

Shallots in a dark, separate
from the perceptive eyes
of russets.

Such a complex matter,
this orchestration of gases
and their effects.

Chilled.
Set on a sill in the sun.
Ripened in a sack
by companion exhalations.

All it takes in the end
is decision
and a sharp knife.

Muriel's Journey Poetry Prize 2021 Winners
COMMUNITY INVOLVEMENT

First Prize Winner & Honorable Mention
Catherine Garrett

Catherine Garrett is a journalist and poet currently living on the unceded traditional territory of the Lheidli T'enneh Nation, colonially known as Prince George. She has been a member of several Vancouver and Victoria spoken word teams, and most recently published in *Room Magazine*. She is an active volunteer with the Vancouver and Victoria slam scenes, often hosting and organizing events. You can find her crying about hockey online at @cath_garrett on Twitter.

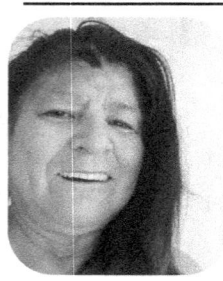

DTES Prize Winner
Dolores Dallas

Dolores Dallas is Cowichan First Nation from Duncan, BC, now living in Vancouver, the unceded territory of the Coast Salish peoples, the Squamish, the Musqueam, and the Tseil-Waututh. Dallas is active in her community in the Downtown Eastside and is a proud Mother, Grandmother, and Great Grandmother. Dallas studied at Spirit Song, a Native theatre school, Native Earth Theatre School, and En'owkin International School of Creative Writing and Fine Arts and has worked with Full Circle Theatre, Vancouver.

Second Prize Winner & Honorable Mention
Michelle Poirier Brown

Michelle Poirier Brown is an internationally published poet and performer, currently living in Lək̓ʷəŋən territory (Victoria, BC). She co-founded the Indigenous Arts and Research Fellowship at the University of Victoria's Centre for Studies in Religion and Society, where she also facilitated reconciliation dialogues. She is an active citizen of the Métis Nation of BC and of Greater Victoria. Her poem "Wake" won *PRISM international*'s Earle Birney Prize in 2019. Other poetry has appeared in numerous magazines and Michelle's debut poetic memoir *You Might Be Sorry You Read This* is forthcoming from the University of Alberta Press in 2022.

Muriel's Journey Poetry Prize 2021 Winners
Community Involvement

Random Selection
joseph a. farina

joseph a. farina is a retired lawyer in Sarnia, Ontario, Canada. Several of his poems have been published in *Quills Canadian Poetry Magazine*, *Ascent*, *Subterranean Blue*, and in *The Tower Poetry Magazine*, *Inscribed*, *The Windsor Review*, and *Boxcar Poetry Review*. His work also appears in the anthologies *Sweet Lemons: Writings with a Sicilian Accent*, *Witness* from Serengeti Press, and *Tamaracks: Canadian Poetry for the 21st Century*. He has had poems published in the U.S. magazines *Mobius*, *Pyramid Arts*, *Arabesques*, *Fiele-Festa*, *Philadelphia Poets*, and *Memoir*, as well as in Silver Birch Press' "Me, at Seventeen" Series. He has had two books of poetry published, *The Cancer Chronicles* and *The Ghosts of Water Street*. He lives on the ancestral land of the Chippewa, Odawa, and Potawatomi peoples, referred to collectively as the Anishinaabeg.

Honourable Mention
Val Davidson

Val Davidson is the owner of Giggy's Beads Boutique. Her traditional name is Misko Mangiikwe/ Red Loon Woman. Valerie is an Anishinaabe First Nations woman from Manitoba living on the traditional, ancestral and unceded territory of the Coast Salish peoples — Sḵwx̱wú7mesh (Squamish), Səl̓ilwətaʔɬ/Selilwitulh (Tsleil-Waututh) and xʷməθkʷəy̓əm (Musqueam) Nations.

Honourable Mention
Jano Klimas

Jano Klimas is a spoken word poet, scientist, writer, and thinker. He first started writing poetry with the Downtown East Side Writers Collective, formerly the Thursdays Writing Collective, in February 2015. He lives on the traditional unceded territory of the Coast Salish peoples, the Squamish, Tsleil-Waututh, and Musqueam nations.

Muriel's Journey Poetry Prize 2021 Winners
Community Involvement

Honourable Mention
Sebastian Yūe

Sebastian is a writer and LGBT+ community advocate of Chinese descent living on the traditional territory of the Syilx People of the Okanagan Nation in Interior BC. They were adopted from China as a baby and the concepts of belonging, destiny, and establishing an identity are common themes in their work. As an educator, Sebastian works to promote tolerance and understanding of LGBT+ populations and has run workshops and spoken at conferences across Turtle Island. They are inspired by space, the stars, and astral bodies beyond the earth's boundaries. Sebastian is an emerging poet and the Muriel's Journey Poetry Prize marks their first poetry publication. You can find them on their website http://sebastianyue.ca and on Twitter @sebastianyue.

Honourable Mention
Gilles Cyrenne

Gilles lives on the unceded territory of the Musqueam, Squamish, and Tsleil-Waututh people. He has published one book of poetry and is working on a second one. He coordinates Downtown Eastside Writers Collective and last year was a co-editor of their book, *Contunuum*. He serves on the board of the Carnegie Community Centre Association, has worked for the last three years for the Heart of the City Festival, and before COVID, taught a course in English Grammar for the UBC Hum Program, a series of free lectures for DTES people who want to return to academic studies.

BILL ARNOTT is the bestselling author of *Gone Viking: A Travel Saga*, and *Gone Viking II: Beyond Boundaries*. He's received *The Miramichi Reader*'s 2021 Very Best Book Award for nonfiction and for his expeditions has been granted a Fellowship at London's Royal Geographical Society. When not trekking with a small pack and journal, Bill can be found making friends on Canada's west coast, where he lives on Musqueam, Squamish, and Tsleil-Waututh land.

WANDA JOHN-KEHEWIN is a Cree writer, originally from Kehewin, Alberta, moved to BC in 1991. Wanda has been a literary performer and publishing poet since 2011 when she picked up her pen again, which she put down when she was 16. She has performed her work at many local events.

ELEE KRALJII GARDINER is the author of two poetry books, *Trauma Head* and *serpentine loop*, and the editor of the anthologies *Against Death: 35 Essays on Living* and *V6A: Writing from Vancouver's Downtown Eastside*. She founded Thursdays Writing Collective, a beloved non-profit organization, and through its ten years she edited and published nine of its anthologies. Originally from Boston, Elee lives on the traditional and unceded territories of the Squamish, Tsleil-Waututh, and Musqueam Peoples, where she works at Vancouver Manuscript Intensive. eleekg.com

JUDGES' STATEMENT

What a privilege it's been to join the talented team that made this year's Muriel's Journey Poetry Prize yet another overwhelming success. Submissions were exceedingly rich in content, authenticity and passion. As judges we read the work blind, not knowing who wrote what, and following hours and days and weeks of review, our judging team came together to collectively make those difficult decisions choosing winners and honourable mentions.

Every contributing writer deserves praise. The work is exceptional. All show insight and ongoing growth in poetic storytelling and content. I know that Muriel is smiling, somewhere, no doubt clapping with exuberance and shared pride. She'd be pleased not only with the writing but perhaps even more with the writers. And knowing that her special journey continues.

Prizewinners and readers were another integral part of the annual Word Vancouver events, another celebratory high point for contributor recognition. As someone who continues to learn and benefit immeasurably from the Downtown Eastside Writers' Collective, it remains humbling to be part of it all.

On behalf of Muriel's Journey Poetry Prize organizers, coordinators, and our amazing community of writers, as we remember Muriel, congratulations to all and thank you for your writing!

Bill Arnott,
Wanda John-Kehewin,
and Elee Kraljii Gardiner

www.ingramcontent.com/pod-product-compliance
Lightning Source LLC
Chambersburg PA
CBHW072040080526
44578CB00007B/545